By Stephanie Anne

Illustrated by Leah Anderson

Illustrated by Leah Anderson

WestBow Press books may be ordered through booksellers or by contacting:

WestBow Press
A Division of Thomas Nelson & Zondervan
1663 Liberty Drive
Bloomington, IN 47403
www.westbowpress.com
1 (866) 928-1240

ISBN: 978-1-9736-4904-5 (sc)
ISBN: 978-1-9736-4905-2 (e)

Library of Congress Control Number: 2018914842

Print information available on the last page.

WestBow Press rev. date: 12/14/2018

WESTBOW
PRESS®
A DIVISION OF THOMAS NELSON
& ZONDERVAN

Inspired by my first grandson Caleb, who once asked me, "Nana, who's God?" Dedicated also to my little angel Alaina. For Bryan and Benjamin, my arrows aimed for Heaven, and for Jesse, Brenna, Grace & Shane, my arrows in Heaven. Acts 26:18

Who is God?

Do you want to know who God is? Let's close our eyes and close our hands, and ask God to help us find out Who He Is. He is right here with us even though we can't see Him with our eyes, we can feel Him in our hearts. He loves us so much, and He wants us to know who He is.

God is our Father who is in Heaven. He is invisible. His Spirit is like a soft wind we feel, but can't see. God is very smart, very strong, and very nice. He is the nicest person in the whole world. God sees us from Heaven, from way up in the sky, past the clouds, from way up near the stars.

Where is God? God is everywhere. He made the whole world, the sun and the moon. He tells them when to come up and when to go down in the sky. He put every star up in the sky and makes them all twinkle so we look up and remember He loves us. He made you and me and all the people, all the animals, all the bugs, bees and birds, the plants, flowers and trees, and all the rivers and lakes. He made the big oceans too. He sends the rain and the snow, the wind, the thunder and lightning.

After it rains, sometimes we can see a rainbow. This is a sign from God, His promise that He will always take care of us. He takes care of the whole world and wants us to help take good care of it too.

What does God look like? He made us to look like Him, so He looks like us! He made each of us very different and there is nobody else in the whole world who is just like me or just like you. He decided a long time ago exactly what color our hair and skin would be. He made us exactly perfect and we are very special to Him.

God had a little boy, a child just like you. He named him Jesus and sent Him to help us find our way to Heaven. His birthday is Christmas.

God gave us His angels too. He sends them from Heaven to help us and to watch out for us when we are at school, or when we are playing, or when we sleep. Angels can see God. Heaven is their home. We can see angels too but only some people have seen them. God said sometimes an angel can even look like a real person. Some people say angels look like bright sunshine. Angels can go anywhere and they can fly as high as an airplane or even over the ocean. They are also very strong, very nice and very fast. Angels really love to sing and it makes them happy when we do too.

Can we talk to God? Yes! This is called Praying. What we feel when we pray is the loving Spirit of God and His son Jesus. We can pray even without talking out loud. God wants us to tell Him when we are happy, or scared, or when we are mad, or when we know we made a mistake, so He can help us. He already knows everything about us, but He wants us to pray to Him. God will always listen no matter where we are. He can hear us even if we don't speak out loud, or even if we don't know what to say. He knows exactly how we feel.

We can pray before we eat food and say "thank you" to God for our food. We can pray before we fall asleep at night, and say "goodnight" to God, or "good morning" when we wake up. We can pray for help when we have trouble at school. We can pray when we see other people having trouble. These prayers make God smile, and He always answers.

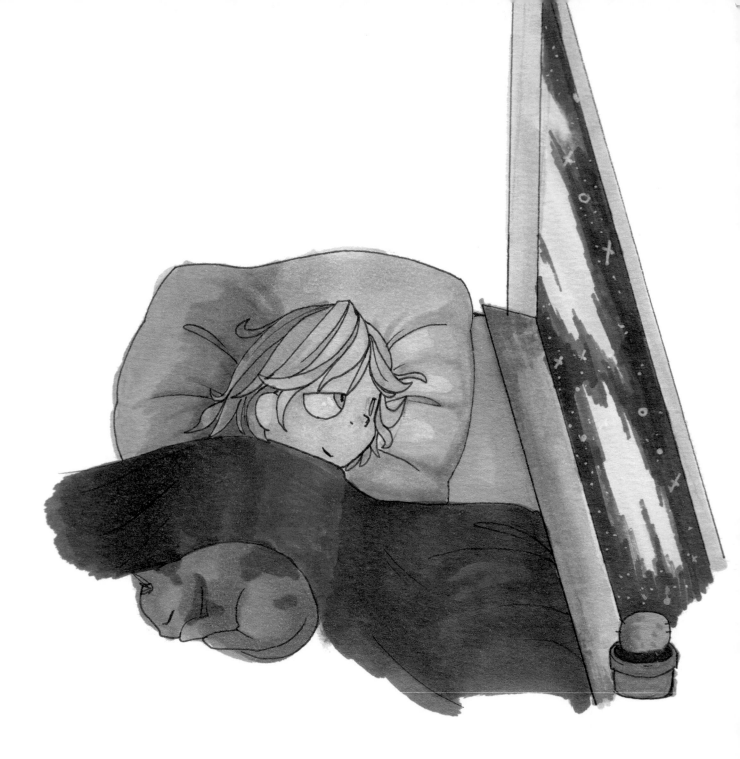

Did you know God makes us sleep? Sleep is a gift He gave all the people so we could rest, and have quiet time, and grow big and strong. When we go to sleep, He never sleeps because He is never tired. He takes care of us while we sleep and He even knows when we wake up.

God never ever leaves us all alone. He is always close to us. He knows we might feel scared sometimes while we are growing up big and strong, and going to school, but He said to try really hard to be brave, and to be nice to other people, and to remember His promise to us that He will always help us. We only need to ask Him what He wants us to do, and then wait and see what He does!

All of God's other promises are in a Book called The Bible, and this book is everywhere in the world.

Nobody is ever really alone because God is next to everyone all the time. And everybody has someone who loves them, because God loves everyone. So now you know who God is...God is Love. And I love you too.

Printed in the United States
By Bookmasters